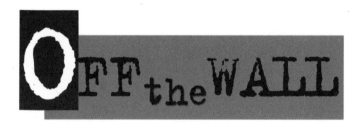

GRAFFITI
for the soul

COLLECTED BY ERNIE J. ZELINSKI

FIREFLY BOOKS

A FIREFLY BOOK

Published by Firefly Books Ltd. 1999

First Printing

Cataloguing in Publication Data

Zelinski, Ernie J. (Ernie John), 1949-
    Off the wall : graffiti for the soul

ISBN 1-55209-311-5

1. Graffiti - Canada 2. Graffiti - United States. I. Dobson, Clive, 1949- .
II. Title

GT3913.15.A2Z44 1999   081   C98-932736-1

Published in Canada in 1999 by
Firefly Books Ltd.
3680 Victoria Park Avenue
Willowdale, Ontario, Canada
M2H 3K1

Published in the United States in 1999 by
Firefly Books (U.S.) Inc.
P.O. Box 1338, Ellicott Station
Buffalo, New York, USA
14205

Design by Interrobang Graphic Design Inc.
Illustrations by Clive Dobson
Printed and bound in Canada by Friesens, Altona, Manitoba

The opinions expressed in this book are those of anonymous graffiti writers and do not necessarily reflect the opinions of the author or the publisher.

The Publisher acknowledges the financial support of the Government of Canada through the Book Publishing Industry Development Program for its publishing activities.

INTRODUCTION

Graffiti is Italian for "scratchings." Evidence of graffiti or scratchings goes back to early Roman and Greek times. Modern graffiti takes many forms and offers interesting social insights, some of which are instantly clear, some of which are maddeningly obscure. For example, in April 1997, as the trial for Timothy J. McVeigh began in Denver, Colorado, for his then alleged role in the Oklahoma bombing, written on the side of a truck in Denver were the words: #*% THE TRIAL FOR McVEIGH. LET US HAVE HIM! The graffiti about McVeigh I can easily comprehend.

However, a lot of graffiti I can't always figure out. For example, on the side of a building on the trendiest street in my hometown of Edmonton, the following is written in bold letters: "De-elect the jug-eared buffoon" (I suspect this is directed at the mayor of the city or the premier of Manitoba). Then there is the famous slogan found at Nantence in Paris in 1968: "*Je suis Marxiste – tendance Groucho.*" I had seen this graffiti in several books and had a pretty good idea what it meant. It wasn't until I was working on this book, however, that I learned from a new source that it actually means "I am Marxist – of the Groucho tendency."

One of the most interesting aspects of any graffiti is who wrote it and why. Who are these unknown people? It goes without saying that some graffiti is not original. It has appeared somewhere else and the graffiti writer has written it in a new place. Graffiti may be an original or modified quotation from an obscure or famous author. For example: "It's alright MA I'm only bleedin" is written on the side of a building on Spadina Avenue in Toronto. This is a line from a song by Bob Dylan. Many of the graffiti scribblers seem to be in tune with the French proverb which says: "If they haven't heard it before, it's original."

This book is a compilation of witty, humorous, inspiring, serious, or just plain ridiculous graffiti. I developed the collection from a notebook of graffiti I have been keeping for some time. I started collecting graffiti for a book I was writing on creativity.

Many people find that the only place they get to be creative is in writing graffiti anonymously on some alley wall or in a public washroom. To illustrate how a lot of graffiti is very creative, I included four pages of it in my book *The Joy of Thinking Big*.

Each piece of graffiti is presented in the style it was written. Some will have incorrect spelling, poor grammar or wrong punctuation. I have not cited the places where I or my sources first spotted the graffiti in this book. Some graffiti I have personally seen on buildings and on washroom walls. Other graffiti I have seen in books. It would be daunting, even impossible, to determine the origins of the graffiti reproduced here.

A number of people have contributed graffiti which they found humorous or interesting. These contributors have been both men and women. A few of the items people have remembered and reconstructed from more than twenty years ago. Most items are from the recent past.

I have divided the material into six categories: general graffiti, graffiti in women's washrooms, graffiti in men's washrooms, graffiti in the workplace, graffiti at universities and colleges, and the gems. The gems are my favorites.

Do I write graffiti? Yes, in fact, I have written about 100 of the more than 800 items that appear in this book. For example, in 1997, I wrote "I Just Want To Be Me—Signed Anonymous" in the men's washroom of the Bistro Praha Restaurant in my hometown. A month later, I checked to see if it was still there. It was; someone had added "Sammy Davis Jr.?"

After revealing this here, I hope the owner of one of my favorite restaurants allows me to come back.

This book is subtitled *Graffiti for the Soul* because I believe that humor is important for the soul. While the majority of the graffiti contained here was chosen for its wit or humor, some items also have an inspiring or serious message.

GRAFFITI *in the workplace*

As a professional speaker specializing in helping people create a balance between work and play, I am interested in good quotations about work and play. Many of these quotations appear in my book *The Joy of Not Working*. It follows then that interesting anonymous comments about the workplace in the form of graffiti catch my attention.

The following graffiti about work come from diverse workplaces ranging from construction sites to corporate buildings. My favorite is the last one about change.

DO IT TOMORROW.
YOU'VE ALREADY MADE ENOUGH
MISTAKES TODAY!

I like my job. It's the work I don't like.

This company's unions are going on strike for the continued right to pretend to work.

Work is what they try to con you to do so that
you will have the money to be able to buy what
they try to con you to think you need.

I am in trouble with the union.
They caught me working.

The day is long.
The pay is small.
So the hell with them all.
I quit!

MANAGEMENT WORK IS FOR WIMPS.

GOD was able to create the earth in only six days because there were no union workers to slow things down.

The productivity of a manager has a lot in common with unemployment.

When pleasure interferes with your work,
give up your work.

When pleasure interferes with your work,
give up your work.

ॐ

Your career is a job you should have quit
a long time ago.

ॐ

Work is an escape for those who have nothing
better to do.

The best thing about working here is
quitting time.

≶

**THE UNION WORKERS AT THIS
PLACE ARE ALWAYS REVOLTING.**

≶

Supervisors stop believing in the work ethic when
they get promoted to their jobs.

Things are bad enough around here without
some management guru coming around
to change things.

§

My job is a big secret.
Even I don't know what I am doing.

§

Ask for a lot from this corporation to wind up
with a little.

We start early in the morning
And work until we have to go to bed.
If this is all there is to living,
We would all rather be dead.

ॐ

THAT RAISE YOU HAVE BEEN EXPECTING IS NOT EXPECTING YOU.

ॐ

You can tell a Union man by his hands.
They are always in his pockets.

You can't blame this company's big mess on one person. This took real teamwork.

PLUMBERS IN ACTION.

(added) Shouldn't Inaction be one word?

Get to know the ropes before you try to pull a few strings around here.

Too much work and no vacation
Deserves at least a minor explanation.
So get your co-workers and raise your glasses
And declare work is the curse of the
drinking classes.

ABOLISH WORK. WORK KILLS!

Manager's plans always degenerate into boring
hard work for us real workers.

It's a good thing for the electricians that they
aren't paid what they are worth.

§

The big potatoes are on top of the heap because
there are a lot of us small potatoes holding them up.

§

We work off our asses
Hoping a raise will come.
No matter how hard we plead
We take no extra money home.

To err is human,
to forgive is not this company's policy.

Things are so depressing around here that the
only people with a smile are those who are proud
of their teeth.

FOR STRESS RELIEF, JUST BANG
YOUR HEAD ON THE WALL THREE
TIMES.

Either Kiss Some Manager's Ass Around Here Or
Kiss Your Promotion Good-bye.

❦

Sexual harassment in this area will not be
reported. However, it will be graded.

❦

Like to meet new people? Like a change?
Like excitement? Like a new job?
Then screw up around here just one more time!

SLACKERS ARE COOL!

My boss's drive is not love, hate, or profit.
It's his need to have me do everything perfect.

The Occupational Safety & Health
Administration has determined that the maximum
safe load capacity on my butt is two persons at
one time – unless I install handrails or safety
straps. As you have already arrived sixth in line to
ride my ass today, please take a number and wait
your turn. Thank you.

You won't get fired by our company. However, you may be a downsized victim of change.

❧

Long daily meetings will continue until we find out why no work is being done.
—Signed General Manager

❧

Working here is a nightmare. You want to wake up and leave but you need the sleep.

Rule 1:   Break every company rule except this one if you want to be creative.

Rule 2:   Ignore Rule 1 if you want to continue working here.

Notice:

This department requires no physical-fitness program. Everyone gets enough exercise jumping to conclusions, flying off the handle, running down the boss, knifing friends in the back, dodging responsibility, and pushing their luck.

When I woke up this morning, I had one nerve left, and now you're getting on it.

✌

THE PEOPLE IN THIS DEPARTMENT WHO ARE TRYING TO GET AHEAD ALL NEED ONE.

✌

If the unions get their work week reduced much more, the workers on their way to work will be meeting themselves returning home.

THE MANAGERS AROUND HERE
HAVE SO MUCH EDUCATION THAT
THEY DON'T HAVE ANY ROOM FOR
BRAINS.

Warning from the Human Resources Dept.
to all personnel: Firings will continue
until morale improves.

GRAFFITI *at Universities and Colleges*

This section focuses on education, and includes graffiti from universities and colleges. My favorite university graffiti was something "created" several years ago when I was taking my engineering degree. I was on my way to the University of Alberta one morning, driving past the Northern Alberta Institute of Technology. The day before, SEASONS GREETINGS had been constructed in big letters on the institute's roof. On this particular morning, GO ENGINEERS had been created from a portion of the letters, the remaining letters discarded. Although I was in the engineering department, I never did find out who was responsible for this prank. Nonetheless, I was impressed with the engineering student who had spotted that GO ENGINEERS could be created from SEASONS GREETINGS.

This section contains graffiti spotted at various colleges and universities. Some of the graffiti poke fun at various faculties; some ridicule the educational institutions' management and faculty; and some ridicule the graffiti writers.

Also in this section, we begin to see graffiti in the "…Rules, OK" form. This style apparently originated in Europe during the 1970s when OK was added to political slogans such as "Provo Rules" referring to the Provisional IRA in Northern Ireland. Over time, this form worked its way into North America and was incorporated into more humorous slogans such as "Astigmatism Rules, OK!" (written in letters four feet tall.)

Who took the fizz out of physics?

§

ARTISTS ARE FIRST DRAFTS
OF HUMAN BEINGS.

§

Einstein Rules Relatively, OK!

§

Education Kills By Degrees.

Originality is the art of concealing your sources.

§

My math professor has more problems than his math book.

§

In law school, your IQ
goes down by 10 every year.

FIVE WORDS COMMONLY SAID
TO A WORKING ARTS GRADUATE:
BIG MAC AND FRIES PLEASE.

Engineering is not a science, it's a disease.

Two law students aren't better than none.

Education students are failed
Engineering students.
(added) Aren't most engineering students
eventually failed engineering students?

§

To make it big time as an Arts graduate,
marry someone with money.

§

The professors in this university seem to have lost
their faculties.

I thought until I discovered university!

ENGINEERS ARE THE ANSWER!
(added) If engineers are the answer, the question
must be really weird.

There are more Computing Science students in
this building than people.

Nothing spoils a party faster than an intellectual
from the Arts Faculty.

❧

Someday I will get smart and leave this place.

❧

EINSTEIN'S REAL DISCOVERY:
TIME = MONEY

❧

Old lawyers never die, they just lose their appeal.

The best way for actors in the Arts Faculty to get practice playing a drunk is to be an engineering student for 4 years.

§

Arts students: write whatever is on your mind. You have nothing to lose.

§

How can these professors measure our intelligence with theirs?

Old accountants never die,
they just lose their balance.

Economists are accountants without personalities.

Arts students have many talents – all trivial.

ENGINEERS KNOW ALL THE
ANGLES.

If you ever need a brain transplant,
get one from an engineer.
You want one that has never been used.

MBAs and economists will lead us
out of prosperity.

Attending university is the opposite of sex.
Even when it's good, it's lousy.

The World Is Flat
—Class of 1491
(added) So are most of the women in our class.
—Class of 1991

S

A tragedy is a busload of law students going
over a cliff with one seat empty.

S

Lawyers should be buried far out at sea because
deep down they're okay.

The degree of creativity is inversely proportional
to the number of engineers involved.

Modern art is buying a painting to cover a
hole in the wall and then deciding that
the hole looks better.

Artists can make practically anything
– except a living.

STICK AROUND THIS BUILDING.
US ENGINEERS WILL LEARN YOU
A BUNCH!

ᔕ

Basic research is pretending you know what you
are doing when you don't.

ᔕ

Learning is what frat rats attempt to do when
there are no parties to go to.

He who can does, he who cannot teaches…
and usually cannot teach.

৯

Old musicians never quit.
They end up decomposing.

৯

At exam time my mind goes AWOL.
(added) Just at exam time?

HISTORY WAS MADE TO BE REWRITTEN.

§

An Arts student going into law is like a mouse studying to be a rat.

§

The purpose of philosophers is to contradict other philosophers.

JOIN OUR CAMPUS BRIDGE CLUB.
YOU CAN JUMP OFF AS EARLY
AS THURSDAY.

❧

The entrances to universities are really wide
and the exits are really narrow.

❧

MBA STANDS FOR
MEANS BUGGER ALL.

Universities teach us to say a little about things
we know nothing about.

Engineering and Science students
hate Arts students because Arts students
are liked by everyone.

There was a young lady named Bright
Who could travel faster than the speed of light.
She started out one day
According to Einstein's relative way
And came back the previous night.

BUSINESS STUDENTS SHOULD
MIND THEIR OWN BUSINESS.

All Engineering students make straight "A"s but
their "B"s are kind of crooked.

It's easy to make a friend at SFU.
What is difficult is to make a stranger.

University is no place to be careless about your appearance. Just miss two or three exams and see what happens.

Engineers suspect that nature played a nasty trick on them but they lack the smarts to really comprehend the severity of the problem.

History Is Something That Never Happened Written By Someone Who Wasn't There.

Am I Bright Or What?
I'm In The Top 97% Of My Class!

If the student is the customer,
And the customer is always right,
They should pass me always,
Even if I am not that bright.

Important discovery just in from
the Psychology Department:
THE MAJORITY OF ACCIDENTS
ARE CAUSED ACCIDENTALLY.

A = Success after graduation
A = X + Y + Z
X = Good Contacts
Y = No Morals
Z = Greed

Euclid was a square.

Free Every Monday To Friday – Knowledge –
Don't Forget To Bring An Empty Container.

Oh, future graduates of this university,
Remember this simple little verse:
To leave this robot factory expecting a job
is dreaming,
To expect one that pays some real coin
is even worse.

My English course taught me that poetry is the
weird stuff in books that has a really hard time
making the margins.

Geography is everywhere.

BEING EDUCATED IS ONE THING. GETTING A JOB IS ANOTHER.

Engineers should use their brains more often.
It's the little things that count.

University education should develop our minds
and not over stuff our memories.

The end of the University term should be closer
to the beginning.

❧

The psychology department is the last refuge
of the insane.

❧

What we university students need is a book called
How to Live on Nothing a Year.

Michael Jordan is a great player
He can jump higher than the hoop.
But he never could make all those baskets
Living at campus on rice, beans and soup.

GRADUATION WILL MAKE YOU BRAIN-DEAD!

What happens if E is not equal to mc^2?

Debating whether Engineers have personalities is
like debating whether zero is a number.

You will leave this university as confused
as when you came here. However,
you will be confused on a much higher level
and about more esoteric things.

Logic dictates that anyone who doesn't know
what to do with their lives becomes a philosopher.

GRAFFITI *in Women's Washrooms*

The March 11, 1996, issue of the *Toronto Star* cites Jane Gadsby, then a master's student in linguistics and anthropology at York University, whose thesis centered on graffiti. Of particular interest to Gadsby is the difference between men's and women's graffiti. She found that men tend to write slogans or statements and women tend to debate. According to Gadsby, women tend to be much wordier than men in writing advice, warnings, and appeals for solidarity. One entry in a women's washroom ran 221 words! Gadsby also found that women tend to write about relationships and feelings more than men.

Although Gadsby found that women tend to debate personal issues, women do write slogans and humorous statements. Following are some of the more interesting of these which have appeared in women's washrooms. None of the lengthy debates have been included since they all were too serious for the tone and character of this book.

If you are wondering whether I spent a lot of time in women's washrooms to acquire graffiti, the answer is no. The items that appear in this section have been supplied by several female friends of mine.

Before you meet your handsome prince you have
to kiss a lot of toads.
(added) While you're dreaming, you may as well
wish for a million dollars.

MY INSANITY IS THE LAST THING I OWN.

Of all my husband's relatives, I like me best.

Women are requested not to have children
in this washroom.

☙

How much did you pay to be poorer today?

☙

HELP, I AM A LESBIAN!

Women's faults are many,
Men have only two:
Everything they say
And everything they do.

§

I like it and him in that order.

§

All men are alike.
They have different faces so you can tell them apart.

I woke up this morning feeling like a new man.

BEAUTY IS ONLY SIN DEEP.

(added) It is better that women have beauty than brains because men see better than they think.

Eve was framed.

All the women complaining about how hard it is to find a husband obviously have never had one.

⟴

Someday my prince will come, but I will have nothing to do with it.

⟴

I wish I could drink like a man
I can take one or two at most
Three puts me under the table
And four puts me under the host.

Women's bodies belong to themselves!
(added) Yes, but don't you believe in sharing?

§

Men who put women on pedestals
don't knock them off.

§

USE CHANEL AND STINK
BEAUTIFUL.

End violence to women, now!
(added) **YES, DEAR!**

One man's Sunday dinner is the better part of one
woman's Sunday wasted.

Virginity is like a balloon – all it takes is
one prick and it's gone.

Don't judge a man by the size of his horn.

IF YOU CATCH A MAN, THROW HIM BACK.

If they can put a man on the moon, why don't they put all of them there?

To resourceful women, men are not the problem; they are the answer.

Boys will be boys, but girls will be women.

Hilary for President
Bill for White House Janitor

⌇

MATERNITY IS FACT, PATERNITY IS OPINION.

⌇

Every Tom, Dick, and Harry thinks he has the biggest Dick.

Join U.S.W.I.S.O.M.W.A.G.M.O.H.O.T.M.
(United Single Women In Search Of Men
Who Aren't Gay, Married, Or Hung-Up On
Their Mothers.)

ॐ

To get to know your husband better, divorce him.

ॐ

Chastity is no big deal if you have never been
asked for a date.

Sometimes you may be the last to know,
That you are the star of the show.

If he is cheating on you, it shows.
Research confirms bad boys have big balls.

Don't put all your eggs in one bastard.

There's three types of lies: lies, damned lies, and those your boyfriend tells you.

℘

Dieting will take the starch out of you.

℘

MEN SHOULD COME WITH INSTRUCTIONS.

Women's word is never done.

❦

Four years of college and whom did it get me?

❦

My last boyfriend believed in every woman
for himself.

A man in the house is worth two in the bush.

Lead me not into temptation.
I can do it on my own.

A HARD MAN IS GOOD TO FIND.

GRAFFITI *in Men's Washrooms*

Graffiti in men's washrooms tends to be more raunchy than graffiti in women's washrooms. Men also tend to write more insults. In keeping with the spirit of the book, I have excluded graffiti of a racist or extremely vulgar nature although it appears in the real world. Some readers may still be offended by graffiti in this section. I have chosen to include these items since they are no more vulgar than what can be found in most high school washrooms.

I bet you I could stop gambling.

෫

I never used to be able to finish anything,
but now I…

෫

I am so horny the crack of dawn better watch it.
(added) Buddy, you better watch it. Dawn is my
girlfriend.

What the hell are you looking at?

≶

A Happy Biker Has A Lot Of Bugs In His Teeth.

≶

NOTHING BEATS SEX WITH MARY
(added) Then why don't you have sex with
NOTHING.

Here at the Rose and Crown,
Everyone is playing a big game.
Sometimes when the bar closes I have Sherry,
And other times I wind up with Jane.

ʂ

Does getting laid in your grave mean sexual
intercourse after death?

ʂ

Alimony is like buying hay for a dead cow.

Constipation is like fishing.
You got to have patience.

◈

I used to kiss her lips but it's all over now.

◈

WORST CHEWING GUM I HAVE
EVER TASTED.

(written on contraceptive vending machine)
(added) I agree, but, Oh! what bubbles!

Press this button for a 40 second speech by
President Clinton.
(written on hand-dryer machine.)

MY DAD CAN BEAT UP YOUR DAD.
(added) Oh yeah! How much would that cost me?

I play golf in the low 70s.
If it's any colder, I come to this bar.

DON'T LOOK UP HERE! THE JOKE IS IN YOUR HANDS!

(written above a urinal)

I'm so unlucky that I even get caught writing on toilet wa....

Some bloke stole my wife.
To get even, I let him keep her.

There was a young lad called McTrabiter
Who had an organ of great diameter
But it was not the size,
That gave women the surprise
Twas his rhythm – Iambic Pentameter

Saying you can have a great relationship
without sex is like saying you can enjoy a Ferrari
without its engine.

The only thing that my mother and father ever
collaborated on was me.

I have twelve inches but I don't use it as a rule.

MASTURBATION RULES, OH...ME!
(added) Masturbation is a waste of
FUCKING time.

Does the lateral coital position mean
having a bit on the side?

My dad says they don't work.
(written on contraceptive vending machine)

Age stiffens the joints and the mind but it forgets
about the thing that really counts.

If I had the wings of a swallow
And the ass of a bloody great crow
I'd fly over Iraq
And shit on Sadam Hussein below.

Blondes have more fun with me because I find
them easier to find in the dark.

I was ruined twice. When I got married
and when I got divorced.
(added) Divorce Costs So Much Because
It's Worth It.

Ah…the American Dream –
Drive a German luxury car, own a Japanese
computer, smoke a Cuban cigar, drink Italian
wine, eat in Korean restaurants and vacation on
the French Riviera with a Scandinavian girlfriend.

REAL ITALIAN MEN DON'T EAT PASTA.

(added) Real Italian Men Eat What The Fuck They Want To Eat!

A little lie can save a whole lot
of explaining to do.

Please, no four letter words written on our walls.
We don't go for that shit.

Women like me because of my size.
(added) It's not the size that counts,
it's how big it is.
(further added) Wrong, it's not how deep you can
plow, it's how long you can keep going around the
field that counts.

EXECUTE GRAFFITI VANDALS

Do It In Concrete And It Will Stay Up Longer.
(added) Stay up even longer with priapism!

Confucius says man with hole in back pocket feels
groovy all day.
(added) Confucius also says man who has hole in
front pocket feels cocky all day.
(further added) Maybe man with hole in front
pocket feels nuts all day.

I PLUGGED FARAH'S FAUCET

If a sheep is a ram,
And a donkey is an ass,
How come a ram in the ass is a goose.

You Are Now Holding Rush Limbaugh
By His Neck.
(written above a urinal)

If you have a chip on your shoulder, it probably
came off your head.

Kentucky Freud Chicken…Mother Fuckin' Good!

I am looking for a serious
and meaningful one night stand.

(added) **NOT ME.**

**ONE NIGHT STANDS ARE MUCH
TOO LONG FOR ME.**

Keep incest in the family!
(added) Keep it out. I don't like anything to do
with my relatives.
(further added) Incest is relatively boring.

Bring flowers to the one you love.
Also – don't forget your wife.

Constipation is the thief of time.
(added) Right, but diarrhea waits for no man.
(further added) You tell them stovepipe.
You've got the hole.

At the People's Pub,
Many of us drink our liquor straight,
Some of us go home with Cathy,
And the rest of us go home with Kate.

Sex at 80 is like having a MSX missile
without a nuclear warhead.

There's three things I look good in – expensive
suits, Ferraris and blondes.

If sex is a pain in the ass, you're doing it wrong.

ORAL SEX IS A MATTER OF TASTE.

Don't trust your wife's judgment.
Look at what she married.

What a bunch of cunning linguists you are.
(at bottom of graffiti filled-wall)

WOMEN GET MINKS THE SAME WAY
MINKS GET MINKS.

I like sadism, necrophilia, and bestiality.
Am I flogging a dead horse?

My kid will beat up yours if yours is an
honors student.

What is the difference between a good girl,
a bad girl, and an evil girl?
A good girl sucks, a bad girl swallows,
and an evil girl gargles.

I avoid all relationships. A "relationship" is when
you're screwing your cousin.

§

**NICE GUYS DON'T FINISH LAST.
THEY FINISH SEVENTH.**

§

Indulge in an orgy once
and you can call yourself adventurous.
Do it twice and you better call yourself a pervert.

Pornography is in the crotch of the beholder.

⸙

I've been single and I've been wed.
And being married cost me a lot more bread.

⸙

Redneck I.Q. Test:
If S.W.C.? = So Who Cares?
Then B.F.D.! = _____!

I've been faithful to my girlfriend several times.

A young, sexy, well-proportioned and
fit woman is the best aphrodisiac.

Sex is occasionally a good substitute
for masturbation.

HELP ME! I DON'T KNOW WHY I AM HERE!

(added) Could it be you were here to pee?

There are only three ways of handling a woman and each one is worse than the other.

Masturbation is the best form of self-expression.

I haven't had sex for so long I think I'm
a virgin again.

❧

God made me a homosexual.
(added) Do you think he could make one for
me too?

❧

The secret to having a good relationship with a
woman is honesty. Once you can fake that,
you've got it made.

The easier it is to pick up a woman,
the harder it is to get rid of her.

JUST DO IT...AND GET THE HELL
OUT OF HERE!

My thirst for fame and fortune was unquenchable
until I started drinking beer.

Bill Clinton Is The Best Fucking President the
U.S. Ever Had.
(added) Bill Clinton is the best President the U.S.
NEVER had.

I was engulfed in total darkness for a long, long
time. Far into the night I saw a warm soothing
light. It came closer and closer and became
brighter and brighter. I experienced warmth
and relief, an almost spiritual experience.
Then the fucking cop hit me on my head
with his flashlight.

The two happiest days of my life were the day I bought my Alfa Romeo and the day I sold my Alfa Romeo.

NEVER DATE A WOMAN WHO CAN BEAT YOU UP!

I came in here just to take a piss and I wound up getting enlightened.

Be sure to read
Random Acts of Anonymity by Me.

You Ain't Having Fun
Until They Have To Dial 911.

the GEMS

This section contains my favorite graffiti. I have found these items the most interesting, humorous, or inspirational. Of course, you might not agree with my choices. No two people look at humor in the same way. Mauro DiPreta, an editor with HarperCollins states:

"Humor is so subjective…you know what humor is like? It's like going to a bad comedy club. You end up poorer and depressed and you think, 'Why didn't I stay home and watch *Seinfeld*?'" I hope you don't feel poorer and depressed after finishing this book.

Mickey Mouse wears a Bill Clinton watch.

My girlfriend likes breakfast in bed and I enjoy
sex on the kitchen table.

I am woman. I am invincible.
And I am pissed off.

Please don't tell my mother I am a lawyer.
She thinks I manage a whore house.

DRIVE CAREFULLY.
DON'T HIT A STUDENT.
WAIT FOR A TEACHER!

If you think it's hot here in Tucson,
wait until you get to your final destination.

I searched into myself and found me.

¤

The worst beer I ever had was stale and way too warm but it still tasted great!

¤

What is Beethoven doing now?
Answer: Decomposing.

¤

Don't leave the haphazard to chance.

Sex is one of my seven reasons for living.
The other six I forgot.

Consider Working For The Lord. The Pay
Is Horrible But You Will Experience
Fringe Benefits Which Are Out Of This World.

MARRIAGE IS A GREAT
INVENTION BUT I STILL
PREFER THE LIGHTBULB.

REPORTER: Mr. Gandhi, What do you
think of Western Civilization?
MR. GANDHI: I think it would be a good idea!

If My Life Was Going Any Slower,
It Would Be Going Backwards.

Keep Breathing. You Never Know When Life
May Be Worth Living Again.

```
I  AM  NOT  OBSESSIVE.
I  AM  NOT  OBSESSIVE.
I  AM  NOT  OBSESSIVE.
I  AM  NOT  OBSESSIVE.
I  AM  NOT  OBSESSIVE.
```

If you think life is a joke, consider the punch line.

To Work is Human;
To Slack Divine.

I'm writing this graffiti, therefore I am.

AVOID DUPLICATION OF
EFFORTS BECAUSE THIS
IS ALREADY BEING DONE BY
OTHERS AROUND HERE.

Does "anal retentive" have a hyphen?

GIVE ME AMBIGUITY OR GIVE ME SOMETHING ELSE.

Make it idiot proof and someone
will make a better idiot.

I killed a six-pack, just to watch it die.

DON'T WAKE UP GRUMPY IF YOU ARE IN BED WITH SNOW WHITE!

§

There was a young lady from Peru
Who went fishing in her canoe
She had a wish
To catch no fish,
Because she was an environmentalist.

§

I am NOT in denial.

Is this in itself a dumb question?
(added) Does Pinocchio Have Wooden Balls?

A well-developed mind
is a terrible thing to waste.
And a well-developed waist
is a terrible thing to mind.

Important Notice To All Arts Students:
Welfare Is Not A Career Opportunity.

Pick any two: Fast   Cheap   Good

```
    I OWE, I OWE,
 SO OFF TO WORK I GO.
```

You Can Always Tell A Male Chauvinist From
Texas. He Thinks "Harass" Is Two Words.

What happens to your lap when you stand up?

Everything in life is an illusion.
(added) Everything…except for illusions. Illusions
can't be illusions if they are already illusions.
That would make them real.

If it's slightly immoral, moderately unethical, or
really fattening – go for it!
(added) Who wrote this? Bill Clinton?

Give a man a fish and he eats for a day.
Teach a man to be a fisherman and he winds up
on welfare.

If a painter is not painting, is he still a painter?

You can never get enough
of what you don't really need.

Down With People Who Are Up All The Time.

This graffiti is dedicated to no one in particular.

PROCRASTINATE AND KEEP UP WITH YESTERDAY.

᭡

Experience a bad spell of the weather right here.

᭡

The future is feminism.
(added) Unreliable, unaccountable, high
maintenance, sometimes pretty to look at,
and usually impossible to deal with.

Life is like riding an elevator. Sometimes someone
pushes your button, sometimes no one does.
Upon entering you get shafted, then you have
your ups and downs. And what is annoying is
encountering all those stupid jerks along the way.

Most of these cliches aren't original.
What we need are some new cliches.

GOD IS DEAD.
(added) Our God is alive;
sorry to hear about yours.

Math and alcohol don't mix.
Please don't drink and derive.
(A message from
Mathematicians Against Drunk Deriving)

If your friends won't leave you alone,
find some new ones who will.

Show me a good loser and I will show you a
REAL loser.

My girlfriend left me,
That I don't mind.
But taking the can opener
Was not very kind.

ᔓ

Don't Look Back Now.
Some Bastard May Be Gaining On You.

ᔓ

Stop trying to be happy
and watch the good times roll.

I am so bored I am going to an opening
of an envelope.

You can never be too paranoid. Someone may be
plotting to make you happy.

While you are wasting your time
reading this silly graffiti, an ambitious
thief is high-jacking your car.

Early to bed and early to rise makes a man dull,
boring, and despised.

If a man is talking in a forest and there are no
women around, is he still wrong?

Lord, make me moral, ethical, and well-behaved,
but not until I'm 60!

HEY DAVID,
SMOKING WILL STUNT
YOUR GROWTH!

Yeah?
Give me one reason
why I should believe you,
Goliath!

ROCK ON!
(added) My sediments, exactly.

Keep breathing. You Never Know When Life
May Be Worth Living Again.

HUMPTY DUMPTY WAS PUSHED.

I gave up hope and feel a lot better now.

I ONCE CLIMBED AN
IMAGINARY MOUNTAIN
BECAUSE IT WASN'T THERE.

Beauty is in the eyes of the beer holder.

"**G**eography is everywhere," says one piece of graffiti. Graffiti seems to be everywhere as well. This section includes graffiti found in public places such as walls in back alleys, front walls of businesses, on fences beside roads, in washrooms, and even on vehicles. Occasionally I have indicated where the graffiti was written if the place has some significance to the item. I have also indicated when a comment has been added in response to something already written.

We should give masochists a fair crack at the whip.

The meek shall inherit the earth…
if that's okay with you.

Really blow your mind. Smoke Dynamite.

If you're in the rat race, remember there is no prize
for outrunning a rat.

PUT UP ONE OF YOUR HANDS AND YOU ARE UNDER A WRIST!

Nostalgia is not what it used to be.
(added) Don't worry. It will be one day.

I am never frustrated,
The reason is quite plain.
If at first I don't succeed,
I don't try again.

Don't clean me. Plant a garden.
(Written on a dirty car)

§

Seventy percent of people are caused by accidents.

§

Procrastination will rule one day, OK!

§

You are where you eat.

```
     HA  HA  HA
     HE  HE  HE
I  AM  THE  PHANTOM  SCRIBBLER
 AND  YOU  CAN'T  CATCH  ME!
```

Jack and Jill went up the hill,
Each with a dollar,
Jill came back with two,
Do you think they went for water?

If Batman Is So Smart, Why Does He Wear His
Shorts Outside His Pants?

Free Charles Manson
(added) With every box of Kellogg's Cornflakes

∽

God is not dead, but alive and well and working on
a much less ambitious project.

∽

FRIES
ACID FR~~EE~~S THE MIND

CLEAN AIR SMELLS FUNNY.

❧

Never cry over spilt milk,
it could have been a can of Miller's.

❧

Isaac Newton was right!
This is the center of Graffiti.

❧

The Upper Crust are a bunch of crumbs
sticking together.

Sex is nobody else's business except for the three
people involved.

When you're dealing with yourself, you are all alone.

The rest of your life begins right here.

I Looked In My Wallet This Morning And Realized
Some Drunk Spent All My Money Last Night!

Whoever said money can't buy happiness doesn't know where to spend it.

ᘒ

A friend in need is history.

ᘒ

SOMETIMES YOU LOSE AND
SOMETIMES YOU BREAK EVEN.

ᘒ

100,000 lemmings can't be wrong.

Tomorrow will be an action replay of today!
(added) **THEN TODAY IS A PREVIEW OF TOMORROW!**

Visit your mother today. Maybe she hasn't had any problems lately.

A Happy Christmas to all our readers.
(on wall of graffiti)

I wonder what will come to be,
In the things that I will never see.
The world keeps rolling on ahead
And the thing that is known as me is dead.

If you do it in a MG, don't boast
about your Triumphs.

DON'T BLAME ME.
I VOTED FOR BART SIMPSON.

It takes about ten years to get used to how old you are.

⟫

You're never alone with schizophrenia.

⟫

Stick up for your dad; he stuck up for you.

⟫

To get back on your feet, just miss three car payments in a row.

I LIKE LIFE. IT'S SOMETHING TO DO WHEN YOU'RE NOT SLEEPING.

Jesus Saves!
(added) How much? As much as the Rockefellers?

Experience is what we call all our screw ups in life.

For a great finish in your internal life, drink varnish.

Marijuana is a thinking person's cigarette.

§

I'll never forget the night I got so drunk I couldn't remember anything.

§

58 percent of all deaths are fatal.

§

Cowardice Rules If You Don't Beat Me Up.

I was married once. Now I only lease.

God grant me the serenity to accept the things
I cannot change, the courage to change the things I
can…and a win in tomorrow's million-dollar lottery.

STAMP OUT GRAFFITI NOW!

WARNING: Phone sex can give
you an ear infection.
(by pay phone)

෴

Miss Piggy is a boar.

෴

I GOT THE URGE TO WRITE
SOMETHING HERE SO I DID!

All lawyers should have a pimp for a brother so
they have someone to look up to.

There was no way. Zen there was.

SMOKE? WHY?

Old sailors never die. They just get a little dingy.

Jo Jo the psychic has just predicted that
your future is ahead of you.
(added) Another startling prediction by Jo Jo:
The future will come one day at a time.

NUDISTS BEWARE!
Your end is in sight.

Today Dan Rather will again bring you the
sequence of events in no particular order.

Advice for all you animal lovers.
Your habits are illegal and disgusting.

Seven out of every ten men write
with a ball-point pen.
The question is:
What do the other three do with it?

Even the most useless person can
serve as a bad example.

Sex is all right but I like the real thing better.

No matter where you go, there you are.
(added) No matter where you leave, there you ain't.
(further added) No matter where you leave, your
absence will be good company.

IT ONLY TAKES A TOUCH OF
GREED TO ACCUMULATE LOTS
OF THINGS.

POINT OF VIEW IS RELATIVE –
SAID PICASSO TO EINSTEIN

Dead people are cool.

SMILE – FRESH AIR IS GOOD
FOR YOUR TEETH!

WARNING TO VISITORS:
Toronto Is The Asshole Capital Of The World.

৯

Bad spellers of the world, Untie!

৯

Count Dracula, Your Bloody Mary is ready.

৯

Reality is a temporary illusion brought about by the
absence of drugs and alcohol.

BACKWARDS SENTENCE THIS
WROTE I YOU CONFUSE TO.

Opportunity knocked and I threw him out.

A PLATONIC RELATIONSHIP IS
AN OXYMORON.

NY ♡ S ME

Starbucks' coffee tastes like dirt because it is ground in the morning.

❧

I want my sanity back and I want it now.

❧

Grass is Mother Nature's way of saying: High!

❧

#*% THE TRIAL FOR MCVEIGH. LET US HAVE HIM!

Ordinary people are the most interesting.

Schizophrenia Rules, OK OK!

DYSLEXIA LURES, KO.

This Graffiti Is Deja Vu all over again.
(added) I think I have read this before.

Diets are nothing but food for thought.

§

I forgot my phone number but it was definitely
into the seven digits.

§

THE OLDER I GET;
THE BETTER I WAS.

Just because everything is different
doesn't mean anything has changed.

Graffiti should be obscene and not heard.

Lately I Have Discovered Reality
And It Doesn't Make Sense.

Four out of five doctors recommend another doctor.

Ha Ha Ha
He He He
Why am I laughing at this stupid Graffiti?
(added) Perhaps you are out of your tree.

I don't like being a masochist because
it makes me feel good.

Go and see Russia and see for yourself
why you shouldn't see it.

᠖

I am too JUNG to see a psychologist.

᠖

PREPARE TO MEET GOD!
(added) Jacket and tie, no jeans.

The writing on this wall is cheap because
supply exceeds demand.

❦

ADAM WAS A ROUGH DRAFT.

❦

Reality is the leading cause of stress
for those in touch with it.

❦

Platonic relationships are meant
for married couples.

Nice guys don't finish last; they just don't fin...

My memory is the thing I forget with.

Schizophrenia beats dining alone.

I'M SCHIZOPHRENIC.
(added) So am I. That makes four of us.

A kick in the ass is a step forward.

Anybody who goes to see a psychiatrist ought to
have his head examined.

Jesus loves you but everyone
else thinks you are a jerk.

Charity begins at home only if you have one.

Illiterates don't have to read this.

❦

EVERYONE WANTS TO BE SOMEWHERE HE ISN'T.

❦

Time is nature's way of keeping everything from happening at once.

❦

Can a blue man sing the whites?

I love this graffiti on this wall.
(added) Don't Wallow In It!

∾

Death is life's answer to the question: Why?

∾

Beware the dangers of making predictions –
especially about the future.

∾

Jack is nimble and Jack is quick.
Jill still prefers the candlestick.

Consideration Rules, If That's OK.

§

I'm not stewped, just inttellecyoually underayted.

§

WATCH THE SPACE BELOW!
(added) Why? What is it doing?

§

Life is a sexually transmitted terminal disease.

Several months have passed,
Since I slept with a woman in bed.
Because I have little money,
Most women think I am dead.

§

There are three types of people in this world.
Those who can count and those who can't.

§

What do you get when you
cross a porcupine with an owl?
Answer: A prick who stays up all night.

The press is free only if you own one.

૬

Sex education is interesting but I never get any homework.

૬

FREE WOMEN!
(added) Where?

૬

There's less to this graffiti than first meets the eye.

If you think nothing is impossible, try yawning
with your mouth closed.

Man, are the times ever a changing;
even the status quo is in flux.

TRENDS GO IN ONE YEAR
AND OUT THE OTHER.

If you can keep your head when all about you are losing theirs, perhaps you have misunderstood the situation.

§

DONALD DUCK IS NOT GOOFY BUT HE'S STILL A QUACK.

§

Vampires are a pain in the neck.

There's no problem so big that it can't be made
bigger with the help of a shrink playing
on your guilt.

If you believe in honest politicians, then you also
believe in celibate brothels.

Monogamy leaves a lot to be desired.

Why is a duck when it flies?
Answer: Because the higher it flies, the much.

Obey all the rules and miss all the fun.

What's the point of exercise and eating well?
You just end up dying healthy.

Preserve Wildlife. Pickle a rodent.

✌

HAVE WIFE, MUST TRAVEL!

✌

Frigid women are cool.

Join the army, see a big part of the world, meet interesting people, and kill them.

§

Reincarnation is making a comeback.
(added) Over my dead body.

§

Of all the things I have lost,
I miss my mind the most.

Sadomasochism means not having to say
you are sorry.

Play the VLTs if you want to get nothing
for something.

STAMP OUT QUICKSAND

James Bond Rules, OOK

※

ANARCHY, NO RULES, OK.

※

The days of the digital clock are numbered.

※

DENNIS RODMAN BULLS, OK.

To all virgins, thanks for nothing.

§

My inferiority complexes aren't as good as yours.
(added) Yes, they are.
(added) You both lose. Texans have the biggest
inferiority complexes.

§

Certainly, it's not certain that
not everything is certain.

This graffiti is art!

(added) THE HELL WITH ART, LET'S DANCE!

There is a dance in this town
every Saturday Night this week.

Roget's Thesaurus dominates, regulates, rules,
OK, all right, adequately.

Kiss is a word invented by poets
to rhyme with bliss.

Drugs and Rock and Roll will help you escape the
crippling grip of reality.

Life is what you stumble into when you've been
expecting much more.

Don't stay away from Church because
there are too many hypocrites there.
There's always room for one more.

YOU MAY BE ENTITLED TO
ROYALTIES IF YOU HAVE
WRITTEN HERE; PAPERBACK
RIGHTS TO THIS WALL HAVE
BEEN SOLD TO PENGUIN.
(added) It's better to write good graffiti
than to sell it.
(further added) Real writers don't write graffiti
unless their careers are in the gutter.

There are three things I can't remember:
names, faces, and I forget the third one.

Paved roads are not what they
are all cracked up to be.

An ethical capitalist is someone who
doesn't shaft you more than once.

A person is known by the company
he deliberately avoids.

THIS SENTENCE IS FALSE.

Shrinks know everything about life except how to enjoy it.

I lost my job, my wife and my Mercedes.
I sure miss that Mercedes.

Boycott Christmas. Santa Clause uses cheap
non-union elf labor.
(added) Don't worry about it. Santa's helpers are
subordinate clauses.

Cannibals don't eat clowns because they
taste funny.

**HISTORIC SITE UNDER
CONSTRUCTION**

We should hang all the extremists!

S

Hypochondria is the one disease that I don't have.

S

OSCAR WAS BORN TO BE WILDE.

EXAMPLES RULE, E.G.

Don't complain about the beer in this bar.
You'll be old and weak yourself some day.

Stamp out vandalism or I will break your windows.

Mind is not matter and matter is…never mind.

PAINT CAN'T STOP PROGRESS;
WELCOME TO THE SECOND
EDITION OF THIS WALL.

Please limit your message to 20 words or less.

A socialist is someone who has nothing and wants
to share it with everyone else.

Am I ignorant or apathetic?
I don't know and I don't care.

God is dead.
—Nietzsche
Nietzsche is dead.
—God

Death is nature's way of telling you to slow down.

⧖

I like to reminisce about the things I haven't done.

⧖

OK, so I'm cured of schizophrenia,
but where am I now when I need me?

THE MEEK SHALL INHERIT THE EARTH

(added) What makes you think they would want it.

Support mental health or I'll kill you.

Celibacy is not an inherited characteristic.
(added) Yes, but death is.

Warning: The last guy who tried to network on this wall got his lights punched out.

❧

Obesity in the U.S. is really widespread.

❧

ARISTOCRATS ARE BUMS WITH MONEY.

❧

Fucque Ewe

Condoms are not as safe as you may think.
I had one on and I got hit by a train.

When I grow up I shall graffiti the ceiling.

Feel Superior. Become A Nun.

Help the police! Beat yourself up!

BILL POSTERS RULES, OK!
(added) Who is this Bill Posters, anyway?

※

If you like games of chance, try marriage.

※

I can't stand intolerance.

※

Bring back the future now.

I'm not prejudiced. I hate everyone equally.

GRAFFITI IS THE ONLY WAY TO ENLIGHTENMENT!

(added) Enlightenment doesn't care
how you get there.

(further added) HOW WILL YOU KNOW
WHEN YOU ARE ENLIGHTENED?

(further added) Enlightenment doesn't exist. It's a
fantasy of liars.

Mickey Mouse is a rat.

What's green and sings?
Answer: Elvis Parsley.

Graffiti's days are numbered.
The writing is on the wall.

Down with gravity!

Nuclear waste fades your genes.
(added) Not mine. They're Calvin Kleins.
(added) Whose is Calvin wearing?
Tommy Hilfiger's.

What's a person like me working
in a place like this?

TAKE GOOD CARE OF YOURSELF.
THE IRS NEEDS A HEALTHY YOU.

Don't be so lazy – write something.

§

Graffiti doesn't grow on walls you know.
(added) IF PEOPLE DON'T WANT TO
WRITE GRAFFITI, NOBODY IS
GOING TO STOP THEM.

§

Orville was right.

I love grils.
(added) You mean girls stupid!
(further added) What about us grils?

§

"I am not surprised," said Columbus,
"To find the world is not flat.
But I am really pissed off,
North America is not on my map."

§

Does any intelligent life live on this earth?
(added) NO, I AM ONLY VISITING!

Gravity is not easy to deal with but it's the law.

BRAS

Women Libbers Should Be Put Behind ~~Bars~~.

All generalizations are dangerous – even this one.

Bart Simpson Doesn't Rule –
He Doesn't Want To.
(added) Bart Simpson is a Democrat.

Bill and Hilary Clinton can't be that rich.
They live in public housing.

In California air pollution is a mist demeanor.

I AM COOL, YOU ARE UGLY.
HAVE A NICE DAY.

The gene pool could use a little chlorine.

If you live within your means,
you're either rich or weird.

§

BE ALERT OR BE ROADKILL!

§

Predestination was doomed to
failure from the start.

§

Inoccuracies Rule, AK.

FREE QUEBEC!
(added) With every purchase.

꿍

Mary had a little lamb and boy was she surprised.

꿍

Sing and shout
And dance for joy,
For I was here before Kilroy.
(added) Alas, my friend, before you spoke,
Kilroy was here, but his pencil broke.

It's hard for me not to write graffiti.
—The Phantom

JESUS SAVES!
(added) Even more than Walmart?

Ban atomic bombs – and not firecrackers!

Join Alcoholics Alias instead of AA and continue drinking without anyone knowing.

❧

Help your local police cut out graffiti. Carry a saw.

❧

I'd give my left arm to be ambidextrous.

❧

If you catch yourself arguing with an idiot, he's doing the same thing.

Charm is telling someone to go to hell in such a way that they look forward to the trip.

CUPIDITY + STUPIDITY = MARRIAGE
(added) Marriage is good for hookers. It provides them with 90% of their business.

Power corrupts. Absolute power is even more fun.

All the world's a stage full of bad actors.

Please help me stop writing on walls.

REPEAL THE LAW OF GRAVITY

(added) There's no such thing as gravity.
The earth sucks.

Dancing Is The Perpendicular Expression
Of A Horizontal Desire.

Always be late! You will be in a better mood than those you keep waiting!

I was born in Australia because my mother wanted me to be near her.

Drink enough of this bar's house wine
and it doesn't matter how bad it is.

I am an optimist. I think all women are bad.

♫

David Letterman has nothing over postal workers.

♫

Van Gogh really wanted to be a piano player –
but he lacked an ear for music.

PROGRESS HAS GONE TOO FAR!

(added) I don't mind progress.
It's change I can't stand.

Roses are red,
Violets are blue,
I am schizophrenic
And so am I.

I LIKE GRAFFITI.

(added) So do I. In fact, I like all Italian food.

§

Clean up your mind – change it now and then.

§

Jesus saves!
(added) But Gretzky tips in the rebound.

SKINHEADS HAVE MORE HAIR THAN BRAINS.

This graffiti will soon be available on CD ROM.

People in Vancouver don't age. They just rust.

Arrange the following words into a
well-known phrase or saying:
OFF PISS

§

An empty taxi stopped and Ronald Reagan got out.

§

Dionne Quintuplets were a hoax.
Five couples were charged in the conspiracy.

Drag down the Joneses to your level and you won't
have to spend so much.

I wrote on this wall because it was there.
(added) I am writing something on this wall
because it isn't there.

SEPARATION RULES, O   K

BACH IN AN HOUR.
OFFENBACH SOONER.

Travel broadens the mind – if you have one when
you leave home.

Badd Spelers Roule, OKay

Pessimists Rule…No Way!

Bird Watching Rules OK.
(added) **FLOCK OFF!**

Fishermen are Reel Men.

Flies spread disease. Keep yours zipped.

MONEY COSTS TOO MUCH!

Love makes the world go around – along with other stupid cliches.

§

The media should get the facts straight before they distort them.

§

Old golfers never die. They just lose their balls.

§

Most librarians are novel lovers.

The status quo is the people who
got us into this big mess.

☙

Not enough is being done for the apathetic.
(added) **WHO CARES?**

☙

MIKE TYSON RULES, KO.

I HAVE 75 BALLS AND DRIVE
WOMEN CRAZY.
I AM BEST KNOWN AS BINGO!

Procrastinate Right Now!

If the opposite of pro is con, then what is the
opposite of progress?

Chicken Man
has a fowl mouth.

§

NONE OF THESE COMMENTS ARE
OFF-THE-WALL.

§

I started out with nothing and
I haven't lost any of it yet.

Every week in New York city ten people are killed,
seven seriously.

꙳

Help keep this country green; plant marijuana.

꙳

I WILL WORSHIP ANY QUICKSAND
SADAM HUSSEIN WALKS ON.

Our school is so violent we play chess
with switchblades.

꒰

When is whoever took them going to give Dennis
Rodman his marbles back?

꒰

If the subway trains were on time,
I wouldn't write on the subway walls.
(added) Blow your nose while you wait for the
trains. You'll get a lot more out of it.

Pyromaniacs of the world, ignite!
(added) Patience needed. Remember Rome
wasn't burnt in a day.
(further added) Patience my ass. Patience is just the
art of concealing one's impatience.

❦

Help! I'm being held prisoner inside this wall.

❦

Roy Rogers was trigger happy.

CRE8TVT RULES, OK.

Teenagers don't need your love. We need your $$.

Why do we drive on parkways and
park on driveways?

Don't eat snails if you like fast food.

§

The early bird is an insomniac.

§

Don't be so open minded that your brains fall out.

§

Where there's smoke, there's grass.

If at first you don't succeed, quit and never admit
that you tried.

CHEER UP!
THE WORST IS YET TO COME!

If the right side of the brain controls the left side of
the body, then only left-handed people are in their
right minds.

Said the potato: I think therefore I yam.

§

If school days are supposed to be the happiest
of days, there can't be too much to look
forward to after this.

§

Life in the yuppie fast lane will get you to the end
in no time.

It's my duty to help my friends get to hell.

Skeptics probably will not rule and that won't be OK.

IF YOU HAVE NOTHING TO DO, PLEASE DON'T DO IT HERE
(added) Space Is Made To Be Occupied!

For Dyslectics Only:
.sdrawkcab ecnetnes siht gnidaer ot ni dekcus teg
reven dluow scitcelsyD

OUR RIVER IS SO POLLUTED
EVEN ATHEISTS CAN
WALK ON IT.

It was a dark and stormy night…
and nothing else happened…

This bar is the home of the dull
and the center of the trivial.

So you think you have it bad. All my imaginary
friends think I am crazy.

BILL STICKERS WILL BE PROSECUTED.

(added) Bill Stickers is innocent. OK!

Old salesmen never die. They just wind up
out of commission.

Choose your rut in life carefully.
You may be in it for the next ten years.

LIFE IS TOUGH. BUT THEN
AGAIN, NEXT TO WHAT?

Indecision rules, O... maybe it doesn't

Humor rules, HA, HA.

Drink wet cement and get really stoned.

SEVERAL ARTISTS HANG OUT
HERE. THEY ALL DRAW
GOVERNMENT CHECKS.

It's un-American to be Canadian.

THE DEVIL MADE ME WRITE THIS.

If your back is against a wall, turn around and let someone write on it.

If everything is coming your way, you are probably on a one way going the wrong way.

Self-help Books Rule…I'm OK…
But You May Not Be OK.

Forrest Gump's biggest problem – he can't see the
trees because of the Forrest.

VOTE BILL CLINTON
FOR EX-PRESIDENT!

Cheer up if you're in lousy shape! You don't have to do anything to maintain your condition.

IF VOTING CHANGED ANYTHING, THEY WOULD MAKE IT ILLEGAL.

I'm glad most people don't recognize me. I'd rather have people know me for myself.

To market, to market,
Some Crack I want to buy,
Home again, home again,
Man, am I good and high.

To protect yourself from nuclear radiation, head
down to your National Public Radio station.
There's no radioactivity there.

MEN SPREAD AIDS!
(added) OK, if you insist.

The only way to prevent what's past is to put a halt
to it before it happens.

What's another word for Thesaurus?
(added) **DINOSAUR, YOU DUMMY!**

The world ends at 10:00 tonight –
on the 11:00 o'clock news.

BEWARE OUR BUS DRIVERS!
THEY HAVE WAYS OF
MAKING YOU WALK.

Sex is just two minutes of weird noises.

I Became Self-Employed
And I Still Have A Jerk For A Boss.

Masochists Rule, Ouch!

Many things rule, etc.

Kilroy Rules, O K

BE ALERT!

(added) Great Idea! Our country needs more lerts.

Palindromes Rule, OKKO

꙳

Vegetarians don't love animals. They hate plants.

꙳

Oh, Jack, you should not do that!
"   "   "   "   "   "   "
"   "   "   "   "   "
"   "   "   "   "
"   "   "   "
"   "   "
"   "
"

MAKE BILL CLINTON WORK, DON'T REELECT HIM!

Insanity is just freewheeling intelligence.

You think you have it bad.
I got addicted to placebos.

Perforation is a rip off.

GOD LOVES YOU
(added) God won't love you for destroying
someone's property by writing on it.

All awning installers run a shady business.

Hashish to hashish
Lust to lust
If the grass doesn't get you,
Then Crack is a must.

ॐ

SEX APPEAL – PLEASE GIVE GENEROUSLY.

ॐ

Egotism is obesity of the head.

Liberate animals.
(added) Animate Liberals.

☙

You can't get anywhere if you think you're
already there.

☙

Read a bestselling novel before Hollywood ruins it.

☙

May smoking cigarettes harm your health.

Never in the history of the world have so few
yuppies screwed up so much for so many.

**NOTHING RISQUÉ,
NOTHING GAINED.**

I can't afford the high standard of living
in this country.

Lassie kills chickens.

What will you do when Jesus comes?
(added) Move Gretzky to right wing.

§

COUNTERFEITERS
MAKE GOOD EXAMPLES.

§

Clairvoyance Is Dead.
(added) I knew you were going to write this.

Twinkle twinkle little light,
How I wonder where I might be tonight,
After over 20 beers I am so high,
Here in this back alley do I lie.

※

Don't Vote! You just encourage them.

※

JOE CAMEL HAS NO MATCH.

Howard Stern is a real phony – I wouldn't believe
him if he admitted that he is a liar.

§

There is a strong connection between body and
mind. I saw a lot of evidence of this
at the post office.

§

If you're not confused, you don't have all the facts.

You think you have it bad. I can't even afford a
nervous breakdown.

PEOPLE IN THIS PUB DON'T
LIKE BEING NOT BACKWARDS.

Bill Clinton is broad minded.

Kilroy Was Here!
(added) I was not. (signed Kilroy)

❦

The Marlboro Man prefers Camels.

❦

Hard work pays off in the future.
Laziness pays off Now!

❦

Golf is an idiot's way of taking it easy.

The biggest mistake you may have made in your
life was taking that first breath of air.

҂

THE BIGGEST CAUSE OF DIVORCE IS MARRIAGE.

҂

IRS agents don't ever quit. They just don't do
anything too taxing anymore.

҂

Absolute zero is cool.

Rush Limbaugh has a narrow mind
but what a wide mouth.

If two can live as cheaply as one,
then why don't they?

Don't be afraid of the future.
It's just as shaky as you are.

Mona Lisa was framed.

I Just Want To Be Me.
—Anonymous

৯

JOGGING IS FOR PEOPLE NOT
SMART ENOUGH TO WATCH TV.

৯

DEATH LASTS TOO LONG.
(added) So does eternity.

৯

Incest is cheap!

ACID CONSUMES 47 TIMES ITS WEIGHT IN EXCESS REALITY.

❦

Repeal the banana.

❦

There is no algebra in real life.

❦

If ignorance is bliss, why isn't 90% of the country happy?

It's not how high you get in life that counts.
It's what sort of drugs you took to get there.

O.J. is i~~nnos~~ i~~nnocs~~ in~~os~~ guilty

Peals of laughter
Screams of joy
I was here before Kilroy.
(added) Shut your mouth
Shut your face
Kilroy built the ruddy place.

Here we have a battle of the wits –
the nit wits and the half-wits.

§

I have been bad and I have been good. I prefer bad.

§

Leather and Whips Rule, Oh Ohhh Kay…!

§

SNOOPY HAS FLEAS.

FRIENDSHIP TEST:

An okay friend will help you move.

A great friend will help you move a body.

(added) A great friend is also someone who is really pissed off at the same person you are pissed off at.

§

WHY ISN'T PHONETICS SPELLED THE WAY IT SOUNDS?

§

"I Love Ewe" said the pervert.

Oh, why don't you work,
Like other men do?
How the hell can I work,
When there's no work to do?

Elvis was here disguised as Kilroy.
(added) Are you sure it wasn't the other
way around?

Help! I was having an out-of-body experience and
someone stole my body. I'm really here. Help!

I wouldn't give a Democrat the sleeves off my vest.

ॐ

Don't Give Advice Here – Sell It If It's Any Good!
(added) Advice is like sex – all right if you don't
have to pay for it.

ॐ

WET PAINT
(added) This is not an instruction.

People are only human.
If this wasn't the case, life would be different.

I'd like to borrow Michael Jordan's body so I could
beat up Dennis Rodman.

I am going to leave this one-horse town once it's
my turn to ride the horse.
(added) Horse power rules, neigh, neigh.

All human beings are born equal.
The trick is to prove one isn't.

PLEASE DO NOT FLUSH WHILE
TRAIN IS IN STATION –
EXCEPT IN PITTSBURGH.

On the street home is where you scratch because
it itches the most.

BACHELORS LEAVE NO RINGS.

✄

The hangman lets us down.
(added) The undertaker is the last man to
let us down.

✄

Curiosity killed the cat but they still suspect it was me.

✄

Be an egotist and be your own best friend.

Something is not necessarily true just because
you experienced it.

§

This Graffiti Could Be Verse.

§

Speak highly of the dead –
thrash them when they are still alive.

§

**NOTHING SUCCEEDS LIKE
MODERATION IN EXCESS.**

It was a dark and stormy night,
The hot air was full of heat.
The river was full of water,
And his boots were full of feet.

If you want to lose a lot of weight,
keep your
big mouth shut.

Government work is organized loafing.

To err is human,
to blame it on someone else is just fine.

❦

**BALANCE YOUR BUDGET —
ROTATE YOUR CREDITORS.**

❦

Snow White was here
but then she just drifted away.

TODAY WILL BE YESTERDAY TOMORROW.

Sadam Hussein buys US Treasury Bills.

Human Beings – What A Stupid Concept!

We should shoot all the jerks who think the programs on TV are harming us.

The problem with Vancouver is the mountains obstruct the scenery.

Support cigarette smoking. It's one good way to get rid of stupid people.

The rapid pace of life is nothing to worry about – the abrupt stop at the end is.

Hey You. Yes You! Just Because Your Face Looks
Like A Hubcap Doesn't Mean You're
A Big Wheel.

I enjoy failure because it can be achieved
with so little effort.

How come no one ever acknowledges me,
For the good things I have done.
No, everyone seems to focus
On how I never mow the lawn.

A cynic is someone who sees things
the way they really are.

∽

Cakes – 66 cents.
Upside down cakes – 99 cents.

∽

ROYCE ROLLS, KO

∽

Texans don't exaggerate. We just think big.

IF YOU DON'T HAVE A DESTINATION, YOU WON'T GET LOST.

You can fool all of the people some of the time and some of the people all of the time – that's all you need to make it big in this world.

Narcissism Rules…Me, Myself and I…OK!

If no one dropped out of grade 9 and 10, who
would there be to hire the university graduates.

I am really bad, this I know.
Because my teachers and parents told me so.

DON'T JUDGE A MAN'S POWER BY
THE SIZE OF HIS EXHAUST.

When in Canada, do as the Canadians do –
be a nice psuedo-American.

I AM LOOKING FORWARD TO THE
NOSTALGIA OF THE FUTURE.
(added) Nostalgia is a boring past filtered through
a bad memory.

Your past is always going to be the way it was.
So stop trying to change it.

Boozers are losers because
all alcoholics are anonymous.
(added) I don't even like drinking. I just drink to
make people like you seem more interesting.

Roget's Thesaurus dominates, regulates, rules,
OK, all right, adequately.

CLEM WAS HERE!

The opposite figure is an example of the mysterious "Clem" who originated in Britain and has appeared in thousands of washrooms across many nations. He has been mistaken for the legendary "Kilroy was here" which originated in the United States and has also had great washroom presence.

Over the years, Kilroy's name has been combined with Clem's picture in North American washrooms so that now most North Americans think Clem is Kilroy. Not so. Clem is Clem and Kilroy is Kilroy.

KILROY WAS NOT HERE!